Raw Till 4

30-Days meal plan - 90 Amazing Recipes to Keep You Healthy

First Edition 2015

ISBN-13: 978-1507575321
ISBN-10: 1507575327

Free Children E-books Club:

I would like to give you FREE GIFT for your child and a full access to my VIP club in which you receive FREE children's e-books once they are published:

Receive Free E-books Here:

http://bit.ly/150k24J

I do this simply because I want my readers to get a lot of value, reach their maximum potential and have a better life. Be the change you want to see in the world!

Introduction

With more and more people concerned by the food they eat, guided by the saying that "you are what you eat", many diets have emerged, some of them having healthy guidelines, some of them doing more damage than good. But amongst all these, one of them truly stands out as being well balanced and combining healthy ingredients as well as good taste and flavor into a diet that can easily turn into a lifestyle and this diet is called *the Raw until 4 diet*.

Also known as RT4, the Raw until 4 diet needs to be seen more as a lifestyle and less as a diet that causes hassle and makes you hate food. The RT4 is a vegan program that focuses on eating as many raw fruits and vegetables as possible, excluding animal products completely and recommending little fat. Raw fruits and vegetables and various combinations are allowed only until 4 in the afternoon. After that hour you can eat a vegan cooked food that is beneficial to your system but with little oil and as little salt as possible.

The RT4 program is not easy for those used to eating meat every day and it can be challenging even for vegans used to cooking their food. But as challenging as it can be, this diet is equally healthy and beneficial for your body and mind, keeping them in harmony and balance, while helping you lose weight or maintain a certain weight. A look at the program's guidelines will show you that it all makes sense. You indulge on as many raw, healthy, nutritious fresh fruits and vegetables until 4pm then you are allowed to cook your food, offering a wide range of allowed ingredients to cook your food with as well.

The real challenge of this diet comes from not eating enough calories. When you eat raw food, you actually need to eat larger quantities to keep you full and give you the needed energy for your daily activities. This is even more important for people who have activities that include physical effort or exercise. Even 10 bananas a day are allowed as long as you eat them in their raw state, combined with other fruits or not. This is the golden rule of this diet – eat as many raw vegetables and fruits during the day, before 4pm!

Below are the main guidelines of this diet, read them through and print them, put them on your fridge and never lose faith in them. They are designed to get your system back on track as long as you have the determination to do so!

1. The diet relies on vegan foods and excludes any animal products without exception.
2. The golden rule is to eat as many raw foods as possible during the day until 4pm then have a high carb dinner. No cooked food is allowed during the day without exceptions.
3. Eat as little oil and fat as possible when cooking.
4. For your cooked meals, the foods allowed include: potatoes, root vegetables, gluten-free pasta, ancient grains and generally most vegetables as long as they are cooked.
5. Avoid using too much salt in your cooking and keep in mind to check labels on canned foods when you use them in your cooking. Shop only for low sodium cans.
6. Green salads are recommended as a side dish for your dinner to aid digestion.

7. No fruits or desserts are allowed after 4pm. If you're craving sweets after dinner it's a sign that you need to eat more fruits during the day.
8. Shop for organic ingredients if you can afford in order to avoid any chemicals found in regular foods.
9. Smoothies are allowed, especially for your morning meal and you can eat as many fruits as you want in the first part of the day. Bananas, berries, citrus fruits, kiwi, mango are just a few of the healthiest and most nutritious fruits that you should include into your daily diet.
10. It is recommended to reserve one day per week for a full raw day. This means replacing your cooked dinner with a raw dinner as well.
11. There is no calorie limit for your meals so no calorie counting is needed. Just keep in mind that raw food has fewer calories than you might think and you will need to eat more raw foods in order to get the needed daily calories. Even more so for people who exercise or have daily activities that include physical efforts.
12. Chickpeas, beans, lentils are allowed but in little quantities as their protein content is higher than their carb content.
13. Drink as much water as possible!
14. Exercise daily. A simple walk each day will help you not necessarily lose weight, but keep your body fit and boost your digestion.

Table Of Content

Introduction

Raw Breakfast Recipes

Goji Pear Breakfast Bars

Raw Lunch Recipes

Gazpacho

Herbed Cashew Zucchini Pasta

Spicy Portobello Steaks

Rainbow Cauliflower Rice

Beet Carpaccio with Citrus Dressing

Tahini Vegetable Salad

Fennel Orange Salad with Marinated Mushrooms

Raw Broccoli Salad

Chickpea Sandwiches with Vegan Raw Bread

Raw Cream of Spinach Soup

Chickpea Stuffed Bell Peppers

Rich Avocado Lime Soup

Pesto Zucchini Pasta

Vegetable Stuffed Avocados

Rice Paper Spring Rolls

Spicy Red Cabbage with Pumpkin Seeds

Portobello Spinach Pizza

Minty Pea Dip

Sun-dried Tomato Paste in Bell Pepper Boats

Parsnip Rice with Fresh Herbs

Cumin Coleslaw

Hemp Butternut Squash Pasta

Summer Squash Cold Soup

Zucchini Vegetable Rolls

Raw Caesar Salad

Guacamole Stuffed Tomatoes

Beet Salad with Parsley Pesto

Spinach Pizza

Raw Lasagna

Hot and Sour Green Salad

Cooked Dinner Recipes

Vegan Coconut Curry

Roasted Vegetable Salad with Spicy Dressing

Vegan Mac'n'Cheese

Roasted Cauliflower and Brussels Sprouts

Quinoa Chickpea Salad

Millet Spinach Soup

Quinoa Edamame Salad

Roasted Bell Pepper Millet Stew

Baked Herbed Falafels

Vegetable Buckwheat Salad

Tomato Caper Linguine

Baked Potatoes with Avocado Garlic Sauce

Quinoa Kale Cakes

Amaranth Tabbouleh

Portobello Steaks with Sautéed Vegetables

Vegetable "Meatloaf"

Mushroom Millet Risotto

Tomato Chili

Spiced Lentil Stew

Quinoa Cauliflower Salad

Caraway Cabbage and Broccoli

Pumpkin Curry Stew

Lentil Tomato Ragu

Bean and Tomato Casserole

Vegetable Soup with Pesto Dressing

Warm Spinach Salad with Raisins and Pine Nuts

Butternut Squash and Tomato Gratin

Quinoa Kale Pilaf

Ginger Chickpea Stew

Asian Style Cauliflower Salad

Conclusion

Raw Breakfast Recipes

Vanilla Chia Date Pudding

Although chia seeds are not as popular as oats, they sure are healthier and more nutritious with their high content of good fats, good proteins, antioxidants and fibers. In addition to this, the recipe also includes dates which are known for their high nutritional profile and natural sweetness. A bowl of this pudding makes an excellent start of the day!

Time: 30 minutes
Servings: 2

Ingredients:
1/3 cup chia seeds
2 cups almonds milk
4 Medjool dates, pitted
1 teaspoon pure vanilla extract

Directions:
1. Mix the almond milk, dates and vanilla in a blender and pulse until smooth.
2. Pour the milk in a bowl and stir in the chia seeds.
3. Cover with plastic wrap and refrigerate for 20 minutes.
4. Serve the chia pudding as fresh as possible.

Chia Pudding with Berry Coulis

This recipe takes the most basic chia pudding and brings it to a whole new level of deliciousness by adding a topping of cashew cream. It's the cashew cream that makes this treat rich and creamy without adding any unhealthy calories.

Time: 30 minutes
Servings: 2-4

Ingredients:
Chia pudding
1/3 cup chia seeds
2 cups almond milk
2 tablespoons agave syrup
1/2 teaspoon ground cardamom
1 teaspoon vanilla extract
Berry coulis:
1 cup fresh or frozen berries
1 teaspoon lemon juice
2 tablespoons date syrup

Directions:
1. To make the chia pudding, combine all the ingredients in a bowl and mix well.
2. Cover the bowl with plastic wrap and refrigerate for 20 minutes.
3. To make the berry coulis, combine all the ingredients in a blender and pulse until smooth.
4. Drizzle the chia pudding with the coulis just before serving.

Apple Cinnamon Porridge

Porridge is the British's version of a morning pudding and it's healthy and filling. A bowl of this in the morning will raise your energy level to its maximum!

Time: 30 minutes
Servings: 2

Ingredients:
4 tablespoons chia seeds
1 cup coconut milk
1 cup almond milk
2 tablespoons date syrup
2 green apples, peeled, cored and diced
1/4 teaspoon cinnamon powder

Directions:
1. Mix the chia seeds with coconut milk and almond milk in a bowl and place in the fridge for 20 minutes.
2. When the chia seeds have soaked most of the liquid, spoon the porridge into 2 individual serving bowls.
3. Top with apple dices, drizzle with maple syrup and sprinkle with cinnamon.
4. Serve the porridge fresh.

Berry Hemp Breakfast Pudding

Hemp seeds are known for their high level of essential fats and they are capable of boosting metabolism and increasing the energy level so they make an excellent choice for your morning meals, especially combined with the fragrant berries which add some extra vitamins and antioxidants.

Time: 10 minutes
Servings: 2

Ingredients:
1 cup frozen mixed berries
1 teaspoon lemon juice
1 cup hemp seeds
1/4 cup almond milk
1 tablespoon agave syrup

Directions:
1. Combine all the ingredients in a blender.
2. Pulse until smooth, at least 1 minute.
3. Spoon the pudding into 2 individual serving bowls or glasses and serve it fresh.

Acai Berry Breakfast Bowl

Nothing compares to a bowl of freshness for your morning meal! Acai berries are the revelation of the last couple of years and their benefits include energy boosting, increasing resistance to viruses, improving mental function and the list can go on. No doubt that these berries, fresh or frozen, are little gems of health.

Time: 15 minutes
Servings: 2

Ingredients:
1 cup almond milk
1 cup acai berries
1/2 cup fresh or frozen blueberries
1 banana, sliced
1 tablespoon raw cocoa nibs
1/2 cup fresh raspberries

Directions:
1. Mix the almond milk, acai berries and blueberries in a blender and pulse until smooth.
2. Pour the mixture into 2 serving bowls.
3. Top each serving with banana slices, raspberries and raw cocoa nibs before serving.

Apple Cereal

This raw breakfast cereal reminds me of granola, but it's quick to mix up in the morning and as long as you have cashew or almond milk on hand, you're up for a delicious and nutritious meal.

Time: 15 minutes
Servings: 2

Ingredients:
2 green apple, cored and diced
2 tablespoons dried cranberries
2 tablespoons pumpkin seeds
2 tablespoons walnuts, chopped
2 tablespoons maple syrup
1 teaspoon flaxseeds
1 pinch cinnamon powder
1 1/2 cups almond milk

Directions:
1. Combine the cranberries, pumpkin seeds, walnuts, maple syrup, flaxseeds, cinnamon and almonds milk in a large bowl.
2. Spoon the mixture into two serving bowls and top with diced apple.
3. Serve the cereal right away.

Fruit Salad with Chia Seeds

As delicious fruit salad is simple, it sure tastes better topped with a few spoonfuls of chia seeds. These small seeds are a bomb of nutrients and combined with fresh fruits they make an excellent morning meal for the entire family.

Time: 20 minutes
Servings: 2-4

Ingredients:
2 apples, peeled and sliced
2 oranges, peeled and cut into segments
1/2 cup fresh or frozen blueberries
1/4 cup golden raisins
1/4 cup coconut flakes
1/4 cup raw almonds, chopped
2 tablespoons chia seeds
3 tablespoons agave syrup
1 lemon, juiced
1/2 teaspoon lemon zest

Directions:
1. First of all, make the dressing of the salad by combining the chia seeds, agave syrup, lemon juice and lemon zest in a bowl.
2. In a different bowl, mix the apples, oranges, blueberries and raisins then add the dressing and mix gently until the fruits are well coated with dressing.
3. Spoon the salad into individual serving bowls and top with coconut flakes and chopped almonds before serving.

Lemonade Smoothie

A glass of lemonade smoothie in the morning is a great way to start the day for two reasons: the smoothie is rich and filling and it will alkalize your body and boost digestion.

Time: 10 minutes
Servings: 2

Ingredients:
1 small lemon, cut into segments
2 ripe bananas
1 celery stalk
1/2 cup dates, pitted
1 1/2 cups water

Directions:
1. Combine all the ingredients in a blender and pulse until smooth.
2. Pour the smoothie in glasses and serve it right away.

Apple and Orange Breakfast Soup

The sound of soup for breakfast may not be that appealing, but this recipe combines apples, oranges and a touch of celery into a real breakfast treat, a soup that is refreshing and nutritious and has plenty of vitamins and antioxidants.

Time: 20 minutes
Servings: 2

Ingredients:
2 red apples, peeled, cored and cubed
2 oranges, cut into segments
1 cup water
2 tablespoons chia seeds
2 tablespoons dates syrup
1 celery stalk, finely chopped

Directions:
1. Combine the apples, oranges, water, chia seeds and dates syrup in a blender.
2. Pulse until smooth and pour the soup into 2 serving bowls.
3. Top with chopped celery and serve the soup fresh.

Fresh Fruit Kabobs

This recipe is piece of cake to make, but so fun to eat! Kids especially tend to love these colorful kabobs.

Time: 20 minutes
Servings: 4

Ingredients:
3 cups fresh strawberries
2 cups seedless grapes
2 green apples, peeled and cubed
2 ripe bananas, sliced
1 mango, peeled and cubed
Wooden sticks
4 mint leaves, finely chopped

Directions:
1. Layer the fruits on wooden sticks and place the kabobs on a platter.
2. Sprinkle with finely chopped mint for a delicate aroma and serve the kabobs fresh with vegan yogurt if you want.

Lettuce Breakfast Salad

Surprisingly, the ingredients of this recipe work together amazingly. The lettuce has a much better taste combined with grapes and an orange dressing and the final salad is refreshing, tangy and nutritious, just what you want early in the morning to kick your day off.

Time: 20 minutes
Servings: 2

Ingredients:
1 small head lettuce, shredded
1 cup seedless grapes, halved
2 oranges, cut into segments
1 cup pineapple cubes
2 tablespoons chia seeds
2 tablespoon lemon juice

Directions:
1. Place the lettuce on a platter. Top with grapes, orange segments and pineapple cubes and mix to evenly distribute the ingredients.
2. Drizzle with lemon juice then sprinkle with chia seeds.
3. Serve the salad fresh.

Grapefruit Orange Soup

If you're feeling bold enough to try new fruits or new flavors, this soup is for you. However, don't think of this soup as a savory, rich dish. Instead, think of it as a refreshing, healthy soup that will kick off your metabolism in the best possible way!

Time: 20 minutes
Servings: 2

Ingredients:
2 red grapefruits, juiced
2 red grapefruits, cut into segments
1 orange, cut into segments
2 tablespoons dates syrup
1 kiwi, sliced

Directions:
1. Mix the grapefruit juice with grapefruit segments and dates syrup into a bowl.
2. Serve the soup as fresh as possible, topped with orange segments and kiwi slices.

Breakfast Three-Ingredient Ice Cream

Who would have thought that you can have ice cream for breakfast?! But you can if you make it using this particular recipe which literally calls for just 3 ingredients. That simple it is!

Time: 4 hours
Servings: 2

Ingredients:
2 ripe bananas, sliced
1 mango, peeled and cubed
1 ripe pear, peeled, cored and cubed

Directions:
1. Place the banana slices, mango cubes and pear cubes in zip lock bags and freeze them at least 3 hours.
2. Once frozen, transfer the fruits in a powerful blender and pulse until smooth and creamy, at least 2 minutes.
3. Serve the ice cream right away or store it in an airtight container in the freezer for up to 4 days.

Cocoa Green Smoothie

No doubt that green smoothies are healthy, but this recipe makes them even better by adding a touch of cocoa powder which is chocolate in its purest form.

Time: 10 minutes
Servings: 2

Ingredients:
2 ripe bananas
1 cup fresh or frozen blueberries
2 cups baby spinach
1 cup water
2 tablespoons raw cocoa powder
2 tablespoons dates syrup
1 tablespoon chia seeds

Directions:
1. Combine all the ingredients in a blender and pulse until smooth.
2. Pour the smoothie in glasses and serve it fresh.

Tropical Hemp Smoothie

Although breakfast is the most important meal of the day, you don't always get to have a full morning meal. This recipe is precisely for those days when you are on a rush and although it doesn't replace a breakfast meal, it will surely provide you with the needed energy to last you until lunch.

Time: 15 minutes
Servings: 2-4

Ingredients:
1 ripe banana
1/2 ripe mango
2 cups almond milk
4 tablespoons hemp seeds

Directions;
1. Combine all the ingredients in a blender.

2. Pulse until smooth then pour the smoothie into serving glasses and serve it as fresh as possible.

Banana Coconut Pancakes

No doubt that pancakes are an excellent morning meal, but what do you do if you're following a raw diet?! Worry not as you don't have to give up on your favorite morning treats! You can make these pancakes which combines the healthy and rich banana with the delicious coconut to create an amazing meal for your mornings!

Time: 6 hours
Servings: 4

Ingredients:
4 ripe bananas, mashed
8 tablespoons dried coconut flakes
Maple syrup for serving

Directions:
1. Combine the mashed bananas with coconut flakes in a bowl.
2. Spoon the mixture on your dehydrator's pan and dehydrate for 4 hours then flip them over and dehydrate 2 additional hours.
3. Serve them topped with maple syrup if you want.

Mixed Fruit Breakfast Bowl

A bowl of this dish in the morning will provide you with enough fibers and energy to keep you going until lunch and beyond. It's a mild, nutritious dish and easy to make; all you have to do is slice and mix and it's done!

Time: 10 minutes
Servings: 2

Ingredients:
1 green apple, cored and cubed
1 ripe pear, cored and cubed
1 ripe bananas, sliced
2 tablespoons hemp seeds
1 tablespoon lemon juice
1 pinch salt

Directions:
1. Combine the fruits, hemp seeds, lemon juice and salt in a bowl.
2. Serve the dish as fresh as possible as it tends to oxidize over time and lose nutrients.

Banana Cilantro Smoothie

This rich and thick smoothie is the perfect choice if you're on a hurry in the morning. It combines the sweetness and richness of banana with cucumber to keep you hydrated and cilantro to pack your system with vitamins.

Time: 10 minutes
Servings: 2

Ingredients:
1 ripe banana
1/2 cup fresh cilantro
2 kale leaves
1/2 cucumber
1/4 ripe avocado
1/2 lime, juiced
1 cup almond milk

Directions:
1. Combine all the ingredients in a blender and pulse until smooth.

2. Pour the drink in glasses and serve it as fresh as possible.

Chocolate Chia Pudding with Mixed Berry Salad

This is the easier breakfast recipe ever! Chia seeds, cocoa powder, almond milk and a touch of natural sweetener are all you need for a nutritious, filling morning meal.

Time: 30 minutes
Servings: 2

Ingredients:
Chocolate chia pudding:
5 tablespoons chia seeds
2 cups almond milk
2 tablespoons cocoa powder
1 tablespoon dates syrup
Mixed berry salad:
1 cup mixed berries, fresh or frozen
1 tablespoon dates syrup
1 teaspoon lemon juice
4 mint leaves, chopped

Directions:
1. Mix all the ingredients in a large bowl.
2. Cover the bowl with plastic wrap and place it in the fridge for 20 minutes to soak up.
3. For the berry salad, combine all the ingredients in a bowl.
4. Serve the pudding chilled, topped with berry salad.

Goji Berry Coconut Porridge

Goji berries have become a food trend lately, but with good reason if we look at their high content of antioxidants, especially vitamin C. In addition to this, they are low in sugar, fat-free and low in calories so what you're waiting for?! Go stack on goji berries for your morning meal!

Time: 10 hours
Servings: 4

Ingredients:
1/4 cup chia seeds
1 1/2 cups coconut flakes
4 cups almond milk
1/4 cup goji berries, chopped
1/2 teaspoon vanilla extract
2 tablespoons dates syrup
1 pinch cinnamon powder
1 ripe mango, diced

Directions:
1. Combine all the ingredients in a bowl.
2. Cover the bowl with plastic wrap and refrigerate the porridge overnight.
3. Serve the porridge chilled, topped with mango dices.

Kale Coconut Granola with Tropical Flavors

What I love about this recipe is that a larger batch can be made at once so you don't have to worry about your morning meal every day or wake up earlier just to have it ready in time before work. Just store the granola in an airtight container and mix it with milk in the morning and your meal is done!

Time: 6 1/2 hours
Servings: 6-8

Ingredients:
1/4 cup water
2 tablespoons dates syrup
1 cup coconut flakes
1 pinch salt
4 cups shredded kale
1 ripe mango, finely sliced
1 banana, sliced
1/4 cup raw cocoa nibs

Directions:
1. Combine water and dates syrup in a bowl and mix well.
2. Mix the coconut flakes, salt, kale, mango, bananas and cocoa nibs in a large bowl then drizzle in the dates mixture.
3. Give it a good mix to make sure the ingredients are evenly distributed and spread the mixture on 2 pans of your dehydrator.
4. Dehydrate the granola at 115F for 6 hours.
5. Store the granola in an airtight container for up to 1 month and serve it with almond milk.

Beet and Hemp Granola

Beets are tiny gems of health with their high content of antioxidants so don't avoid them. Even morning meals can include a small serving of beets as they will boost your energy level and fill you up with vitamins for the entire day ahead. The strawberries boost the aroma, as well as the nutritional profile.

Time: 6 1/2 hours
Servings: 4-6

Ingredients:
1 cup hemp seeds
1/4 cup dried cranberries
1 large beet, cut into very fine slices
1 cup fresh strawberries, sliced
1/2 cup pitted dates, chopped
1/2 cup water
1/2 teaspoon cinnamon powder

Directions:
1. Combine the hemp seeds, cranberries, beet slices, strawberries and pitted dates in a bowl.
2. Stir in the water then sprinkle with cinnamon and mix until evenly distributed.
3. Spread the mixture over the pans of your dehydrator and dehydrate the granola at 115F for 6 hours.
4. Store in an airtight container for up to 1 month and serve it with coconut milk, almond milk and maple syrup.

Tropical Lime Pudding

This tangy pudding and its tropical aroma is your best choice for breakfast if you prefer light, refreshing flavors.

Time: 15 minutes
Servings: 2

Ingredients:
1 ripe mango
2 tablespoons hemp seeds
1 teaspoon lime zest
Juice from 1 lime
2 tablespoons date syrup
2 mint leaves
2 tablespoons coconut flakes

Directions:
1. Combine all the ingredients, except coconut flakes, in a blender.
2. Pulse until the pudding is smooth then spoon it into serving bowls.
3. Top the pudding with coconut flakes just before serving.

Kale Banana Wraps

These morning wraps are easy to make, but so healthy! Bananas, kale, chia seeds and almond butter are just a few of the ingredients of this wraps, but keep in mind that they can easily be customized to your likings and needs.

Time: 15 minutes
Servings: 4

Ingredients:
4 kale leaves
2 tablespoons almond butter
2 ripe bananas, sliced
2 tablespoons dates syrup
4 tablespoons chia seeds

Directions:
1. Place the kale leaves on your working surface.
2. Spread almond butter over each kale leaf then top them with banana slices.
3. Drizzle with maple syrup and sprinkle with chia seeds.
4. Wrap the kale wraps tightly and serve the wraps fresh.

Coconut Blueberry Yogurt

Dairy may not be vegan and gluten free, but cashews make an excellent replacement for dairies and you can even make cheese or yogurt using cashew nuts. And this recipe is the perfect example!

Time: 15 minutes
Servings: 2

Ingredients:
Flesh from 1 fresh coconut
1/2 cup water
1 ripe banana
1 cup fresh or frozen blueberries
2 tablespoons lemon juice
2 tablespoons dates syrup

Directions:
1. Mix all the ingredients in a blender and pulse until smooth. It might take a few minutes until the mixture smoothens up.
2. Pour the yogurt into individual serving cups and serve it preferably fresh.

Raw Spiced Fig Compote

Although compote may not sound like a good breakfast choice, this version sure is! It's refreshing but filling and nutritious and it uses figs which are incredibly healthy.

Time: 20 minutes
Servings: 2

Ingredients:
8 fresh figs, quartered
2 tablespoons dates syrup
1/2 cup water
1 star anise
1/4 cup walnuts, chopped
1/4 cup millet flakes

Directions:
1. Combine the figs, dates syrup, water and star anise in a bowl.
2. Cover the bowl with plastic wrap and refrigerate for 1 hour.
3. Top with walnuts and millet flakes and serve immediately.

Persimmon Chia Custard

Although persimmon is not as common as oranges or apples, it sure is a healthy fruit, loaded with vitamins, antioxidants and fibers and having a mild taste. This recipe uses it in its raw state so you get to take advantages of all its benefits while enjoying a delicious, one-of-a-kind custard.

Time: 15 minutes
Servings: 2

Ingredients:
2 ripe persimmons
2 tablespoons dates syrup
1/2 teaspoon vanilla extract
2 tablespoons coconut cream
2 tablespoons chia seeds

Directions:
1. Peel the persimmons and place them in a food processor or blender.
2. Add the dates syrup, vanilla, coconut cream and pulse until smooth.
3. Stir in the chia seeds and mix well.
4. Spoon the custard into 2 serving glasses and serve it chilled.

Berry Smoothie Breakfast Bowl

This smoothie bowl is a mix between the deliciousness of a smoothie and the nutrients of a healthy morning meal – all into one bowl!

Time: 15 minutes
Servings: 2

Ingredients:
1 ripe banana
1 cup frozen berries
1 1/2 cups almond milk
2 tablespoons coconut flakes
2 tablespoons almond slices
2 tablespoons sunflower seeds
1 cup fresh raspberries

Directions:
1. Mix the banana, frozen berries and almond milk in a blender and pulse until smooth.
2. Pour the smoothie into 2 breakfast bowls.
3. Top each bowl with coconut flakes, almond slices, sunflower seeds and fresh raspberries and serve as fresh as possible.

Banana Hazelnut Celery Logs

These celery logs are so fun to make! The hazelnut filling is delicious on its own, but in this combination it brings everything together perfectly.

Time: 20 minutes
Servings: 4

Ingredients:
1/4 cup hazelnuts
1/2 cup dates, pitted
2 tablespoons cocoa powder
1 pinch salt
1/4 cup water
4 celery stalks
2 ripe bananas, sliced

Directions:
1. Combine the hazelnuts, dates, cocoa powder, salt and water in a blender and pulse until smooth.
2. Place the celery stalks on a platter then carefully spoon the hazelnut mix into each log.
3. Top the celery with banana slices and serve them fresh.

Goji Pear Breakfast Bars

These tiny red fruits named goji are bombs of antioxidants and health so if you happen to find them when you go shopping, do put them in your shopping cart and make these breakfast bars for a delicious, nutritious start of the day.

Time: 5 hours
Servings: 12

Ingredients:
1 1/2 cups dates, pitted
1/2 cup pumpkin seeds, soaked overnight
1 1/2 cup ground flaxseeds
1 1/2 cups water
1/2 cup goji berries
1/4 cup cocoa powder
1/4 teaspoon cinnamon powder
1/4 teaspoon ground ginger
2 ripe pears, diced

Directions:
1. Combine the ground flaxseeds and water in a bowl and let them soak up for 10 minutes.
2. Mix the dates with pumpkin seeds in a food processor.
3. Stir in the ground flaxseeds, then add the goji berries, cocoa powder, cinnamon and ginger.
4. Spoon the mixture into the pan of your dehydrator, leveling it up into 1 1/2-inch thick sheet. Top with pear dices and dehydrate at 145F for 45 minutes. Reduce the heat to 115F and dehydrate 4 additional hours. You want the bars to be dry, but not brittle.
5. Cut into small bars and serve fresh or store in an airtight container for up to 1 week.

Raw Lunch Recipes

Gazpacho

Gazpacho is a classic raw soup that combines a wide range of vegetables to create a refreshing and yet filling soup.

Time: 25 minutes
Servings: 2-4

Ingredients:
4 ripe tomatoes, peeled
4 sun-dried tomatoes
2 garlic cloves
1 shallot
1 cup water
2 tablespoons olive oil

2 tablespoons lemon juice
2 basil leaves
Salt and pepper to taste

Directions:
1. Combine all the ingredients in a food processor and pulse until well mixed.
2. Pour the soup in bowls and serve it as fresh as possible.

Herbed Cashew Zucchini Pasta

Zucchini pasta is a great replacer for regular, traditional pasta. It's lighter and much healthier and the cashew sauce makes it creamy and so flavorful. For lunch, this is definitely a strong choice!

Time: 30 minutes
Servings: 4

Ingredients:
4 young zucchinis
1 cup cashew nuts, soaked overnight
1/4 cup coconut milk
1/4 cup basil leaves
1/4 cup parsley leaves
2 tablespoons pine nuts
Salt and pepper to taste
1 pinch chili flakes
2 tablespoons olive oil

Directions:
1. Using a spiral slicer, cut the zucchini into fine threads, forming the pasta.
2. Combine the cashew nuts, coconut milk, basil, parsley, pine nuts, chili flakes, salt and pepper in a powerful blender.
3. Pulse until the sauce is creamy and smooth then combine it with the zucchini pasta.
4. Spoon the pasta into serving bowls and serve it fresh, drizzled with a touch of olive oil.

Spicy Portobello Steaks

Vegans may not eat meat, but they have plenty of protein sources in exchange, mushrooms being one of them. More so for raw mushrooms, like these spicy Portobello steaks which are not only healthy, but also incredibly fragrant and delicious!

Time: 30 minutes
Servings: 4

Ingredients:
4 Portobello mushrooms
2 tablespoons olive oil
2 tablespoons balsamic vinegar
1 tablespoon coconut aminos
Salt and pepper to taste
1/2 teaspoon chili flakes

Directions:
1. Mix the olive oil with balsamic vinegar, coconut aminos, chili flakes, salt and pepper in a bowl.
2. Cut the mushrooms into quarters and place them in a bowl.
3. Drizzle the mushrooms with the olive oil mixture and let them marinate for 20 minutes in the fridge.
4. Serve the mushrooms fresh.

Rainbow Cauliflower Rice

Cauliflower is one of the best vegetables out there for vegans. In its raw form it has a mild taste and that allows vegans to use it as a base for many dishes, including this rice-like dish.

Time: 30 minutes
Servings: 4-6

Ingredients:
1 head cauliflower, cut into florets
1 red bell pepper, cored and diced
1 yellow bell pepper, cored and diced
1 green bell pepper, cored and diced
1 cucumber, diced
2 tomatoes, seeded and diced
1/2 cup chopped parsley
2 tablespoons pine nuts
Salt and pepper to taste
2 tablespoons olive oil
2 tablespoons lemon juice

Directions:
1. Place the cauliflower florets in a food processor and pulse until ground, but not fine.
2. Transfer the cauliflower into a bowl and stir in the remaining ingredients.
3. Season the "rice" with salt and pepper and serve it fresh or store in the fridge for 1 day.

Beet Carpaccio with Citrus Dressing

Beets and their bright purple color are incredibly healthy. Their color itself is a statement of their high content of antioxidants. Consuming them raw can become a healthy routine in your diet and recipes like this carpaccio surely emphasize the natural aroma of beets without allowing it to take over your taste buds.

Time: 30 minutes
Servings: 2-4

Ingredients:
3 small beets
2 cups arugula leaves
1 small avocado, peeled and sliced
2 tablespoons lemon juice
2 tablespoons orange juice
1 teaspoon lemon zest
2 tablespoons olive oil
Salt and pepper to taste

Directions:
1. Peel and cut the beets into thin slices. Place them on a salad platter.
2. Top the beets with arugula leaves and avocado slices.
3. Mix the lemon juice, orange juice, lemon zest, salt and pepper in a glass jar. Cover with a lid and shake until smooth.
4. Drizzle this dressing over the beet carpaccio.
5. Serve the carpaccio as fresh as possible.

Tahini Vegetable Salad

Kale is not exactly the softest vegetable to eat raw, but here the trick: remove the stems of the leaves and combine the kale with a creamy dressing and you've got yourself a great lunch meal!

Time: 20 minutes
Servings: 2-4

Ingredients:
1 bunch kale leaves, stems removed and shredded
2 celery stalks, sliced
2 cups broccoli florets
1/2 avocado, mashed
2 tablespoons tahini paste
3 tablespoons lemon juice
Salt and pepper to taste

Directions:
1. Mix the avocado, lemon juice, salt and pepper in a blender and pulse until smooth.
2. Combine the kale, celery and apples with the smooth dressing and mix gently.
3. Serve the salad as fresh as possible.

Fennel Orange Salad with Marinated Mushrooms

Fennel is an intensely flavored vegetable and for that reason not everyone likes it. But citrus fruits tame its aroma well so this salad is well balanced and delicious!

Time: 25 minutes
Servings: 4

Ingredients:
Fennel salad:
1 fennel bulb, finely sliced
2 oranges, cut into segments
4 radishes, finely sliced
1 carrot, cut into thin strips
2 tablespoons lemon juice
Salt and pepper to taste
Marinated Portobello:
4 Portobello mushrooms
2 tablespoons lemon juice
2 tablespoons coconut aminos
1 teaspoon tamarind paste

Directions:
1. Mix the lemon juice, coconut aminos and tamarind paste in a bowl. Brush the mushrooms with this mixture and let them marinate until the salad is ready.
2. Combine the fennel, oranges, radishes and carrot in a salad bowl.
3. Add the lemon juice, salt and pepper and mix gently.
4. Serve the mushrooms topped with plenty of salad.

Raw Broccoli Salad

Many people find broccoli to be tasting better in its raw form rather than cooked and the truth is that when not cooked, broccoli preserves its nutrients and fibers and it's much healthier consumed this way than cooked.

Time: 25 minutes
Servings: 4

Ingredients:
1 small head broccoli, cut into florets
3 cups baby spinach
2 cucumbers, sliced
1 avocado, sliced
2 green onions, coarsely chopped
1/2 lemon, juiced
Salt and pepper to taste

Directions:
1. Combine the broccoli, baby spinach, avocado, cucumbers and green onions in a salad bowl.
2. Drizzle with lemon juice then add salt and pepper to taste.
3. Serve the salad fresh.

Chickpea Sandwiches with Vegan Raw Bread

Considering how filling these sandwiches are, this dish can easily become your lunch meal. The bread can also be used for other purposes, not just for sandwiches.

Time: 8 1/2 hours
Servings: 6-8

Ingredients:
Vegan raw bread:
2 young zucchinis, cubed
1 tomato
1 shallot, chopped
1/4 cup sun-dried tomatoes
1 cup ground flax seeds
2 tablespoons chia seeds
Salt and pepper to taste
Chickpea spread:
2 cups sprouted chickpeas
1/4 cup water
2 tablespoons lemon juice
2 tablespoons tahini paste
2 green onions, chopped
Salt and pepper to taste
Arugula and sliced tomatoes to make the sandwiches

Directions:
1. To make the bread, mix the zucchinis, tomato, shallot, sun-dried tomatoes and flax seeds in a food processor.
2. Pulse until well mixed then add the remaining ingredients.
3. Spoon the mixture into the pan of your dehydrator, making sure it's about 1/2-inch thick all the way.
4. Place in thee dehydrator and dehydrate at 115F for 7 hours.
5. To make the spread, combine the chickpeas, water, lemon juice, tahini paste, salt and pepper in a powerful blender.
6. Pulse until smooth then fold in the green onions.
7. To make the sandwiches, cut the bread into squares. Spread each square with chickpea spread and sandwich them together two by two with arugula and sliced tomatoes.

Raw Cream of Spinach Soup

Spinach is surely not amongst your top three favorite veggies, but this soup is well worth a try despite that. Not only because it's incredibly tasty, but also because the extra ingredients of this soup make it mild and delicious!

Time: 20 minutes
Servings: 4

Ingredients:
3 cups baby spinach
2 cucumbers, peeled
1/4 cup cashew nuts, soaked overnight
2 tablespoons lemon juice
2 mint leaves
1 cup coconut milk
Salt and pepper to taste
Ice cubes

Directions:
1. Combine all the ingredients in a blender and pulse until smooth.
2. Season with salt and pepper to taste and serve the soup as fresh as possible.
3. Add 2 cubes of ice in each serving bowl for a more intense taste.

Chickpea Stuffed Bell Peppers

These stuffed bell peppers are incredibly versatile. This version uses chickpeas as a filling, but other vegetables or even cashew nuts or herbs can become filling.

Time: 30 minutes
Servings: 4

Ingredients:
4 red bell peppers
2 cups sprouted chickpeas
1/2 cup cashew nuts, soaked overnight
1/4 cup sunflower seeds
2 tablespoon lemon juice
1 tablespoon olive oil
Salt and pepper to taste
2 green onions, chopped
1 celery stalk, chopped

Directions:
1. Cut the top of each bell pepper and carefully remove the core.
2. In a food processor, mix the cashew nuts, sunflower seeds, lemon juice and olive oil. Pulse until well mixed then add salt and pepper.
3. Stir in the green onions and celery then spoon the filling into each bell pepper.
4. Serve the bell peppers fresh.

Rich Avocado Lime Soup

The richness of this avocado soup is impressive. Such a simple recipe and yet the result is outstanding and incredibly healthy with its high content of good fats and fibers.

Time: 20 minutes
Servings: 4

Ingredients:
2 ripe avocados
2 cucumbers, peeled
1 cup chilled water
1 celery stalk
1 lime, juiced
1/2 teaspoon cumin seeds
1/4 cup coriander leaves
Salt and pepper to taste
2 tablespoons pumpkin seeds

Directions:
1. Combine the avocados, cucumbers, water, celery, lime juice, cumin seeds, coriander, salt and pepper in a blender and pulse until smooth.
2. Pour the soup into serving bowls and top with a few pumpkin seeds.

Pesto Zucchini Pasta

Pesto is a well know Italian sauce that uses basil as its main ingredient, therefore it has an intense taste and aroma. It makes an excellent complementary sauce for these delicate zucchini pasta.

Time: 20 minutes
Servings: 4

Ingredients:
4 young zucchinis
1 cup fresh basil leaves
4 garlic cloves
1/4 cup pine nuts
2 tablespoons lemon juice
Salt and pepper to taste

Directions:
1. Mix the basil, garlic, lemon juice and pine nuts in a blender and pulse until smooth. Add 1-2 tablespoons of water if the mixture doesn't come together or needs to be thinned down slightly.
2. Add salt and pepper to taste.
3. Cut the zucchinis with a spiral cutter into fine threads or use a vegetable peeler to cut them into thin strips.
4. Place the zucchinis in a bowl and stir in the pesto.
5. Serve the pasta fresh.

Vegetable Stuffed Avocados

Although at its base this recipe is a salad, serving it in the avocado skins makes it far more appealing for the eye. As for its taste, a look at the ingredient list will convince you of its flavor and nutritious benefits.

Time: 20 minutes
Servings: 4

Ingredients:
2 ripe avocados
2 ripe tomatoes, diced
2 garlic cloves, minced
1 shallot, chopped
2 green onions, chopped
1/2 cup chopped parsley
1/2 lemon, juiced
Salt and pepper to taste
2 tablespoons hemp seeds

Directions:
1. Cut the avocados in half and carefully remove the flesh, leaving the skins intact.
2. Mash the avocados with a fork and stir in the remaining ingredients.
3. Adjust the taste with salt and pepper and spoon the salad into the avocado skins.
4. Serve the dish as fresh as possible, sprinkled with hemp seeds.

Rice Paper Spring Rolls

Gotta love these fresh, nutritious rolls! Made with only raw ingredients and served with a lemon dressing, they are small bundles of deliciousness and freshness.

Time: 30 minutes
Servings: 4

Ingredients:
4 rice papers (or lettuce leaves)
2 carrots, cut into thin sticks
1/2 cup sprouted chickpeas
1/2 cup shredded red cabbage
1 small cucumber, cut into sticks
1 avocado, sliced
2 tablespoons dates syrup
2 tablespoons lemon juice
1 small red pepper, seeded and chopped
2 tablespoons tomato sauce
Salt and pepper to taste

Directions:
1. Mix the dates syrup, lemon juice, red pepper and tomato sauce in a small bowl. Add salt and pepper to taste.

2. Lay the lettuce leaves on your chopping board.
3. Place the chickpeas, red cabbage, cucumber and avocado slices on each lettuce leaves.
4. Roll the lettuce leaves tightly.
5. Serve the rolls dipped in the vinegar sauce made earlier.

Spicy Red Cabbage with Pumpkin Seeds

How could you say no to a bowl of spicy red cabbage, topped with a crunchy pumpkin seed mixture?! It's such a delicious and texturized dish to have for your lunch!

Time: 30 minutes
Servings: 4

Ingredients:
4 cups shredded red cabbage
1/2 cup chopped cilantro
2 tablespoons lemon juice
2 garlic cloves, minced
1 lime, juiced
1/2 teaspoon sesame oil
1 tablespoon olive oil
1/2 cup pumpkin seeds
1/2 red pepper, seeded and chopped
Salt and pepper to taste

Directions:
1. Combine the cabbage with cilantro, balsamic vinegar, garlic, lime juice and sesame oil in a salad bowl.
2. Add salt and pepper to taste.
3. For the topping, mix the pumpkin seeds with olive oil and red pepper.
4. Top the salad with the pumpkin seed mixture and serve immediately.

Portobello Spinach Pizza

Traditional pizza is time consuming, unlike this raw Portobello pizza which is done in no time and tastes like no other!

Time: 15 minutes
Servings: 4

Ingredients:
4 large Portobello mushrooms
1 cup baby spinach
1/2 cup cherry tomatoes, halved
1/4 cup black olives, pitted
4 sun-dried tomatoes
2 tablespoons olive oil
2 garlic cloves
2 tablespoons lemon juice
Salt and pepper to taste

Directions:
1. Place the mushrooms on a platter.
2. Top each mushroom with baby spinach, cherry tomatoes and black olives.
3. Mix the sun-dried tomatoes, olive oil, garlic and lemon juice in a mortar and crush them with a pestle until smooth.
4. Drizzle the dressing over the mushrooms and serve the pizzas fresh.

Minty Pea Dip

Despite having only a few ingredients, this dip is delicious and nutritious and at the same time refreshing. Serve it with slices of cucumber or even lettuce leaves to keep it all the way through raw and you're up for a simple and amazing meal for lunch!

Time: 15 minutes
Servings: 2-4

Ingredients:
3 cups green peas
3 tablespoons lemon juice
1 garlic clove
6 fresh mint leaves
2 tablespoons tahini paste
Salt and pepper to taste
2 tablespoons pine nuts

Directions:

1. Combine all the ingredients in a blender or food processor and pulse until smooth.
2. Spoon the dip into a serving bowl and serve it as fresh as possible. If needed, store in the fridge covered with plastic wrap.

Sun-dried Tomato Paste in Bell Pepper Boats

This pate packs the flavors of summer tomatoes in just one spoonful. It's such a delicious and flavorful dip, perfect with vegetable sticks or vegan bread!

Time: 15 minutes
Servings: 4

Ingredients:
1 1/2 cups sun-dried tomatoes
1/2 cup sunflower seeds
1 tablespoon lemon juice
2 garlic cloves
1 teaspoon dried basil
1/2 teaspoon dried oregano
Salt and pepper to taste
2 yellow bell peppers, halved
1 tablespoon chia seeds

Directions:
1. Combine all the ingredients in a blender or food processor and pulse until smooth.
2. Add salt and pepper to taste and mix well.
3. Remove the core and veins from each bell pepper.
4. Spoon the sun-dried tomato paste into each bell pepper half and top with a sprinkle of chia seeds.
5. Serve them fresh.

Parsnip Rice with Fresh Herbs

Fine parsnip rice combines with the fresh flavor of herbs and green peas in this bright, aromatic lunch. Despite its look and ingredients, this dish is well balanced and filling.

Time: 20 minutes
Servings: 2-4

Ingredients:
1 pound parsnips, peeled and chopped
1 cup chopped parsley
1 cup chopped cilantro
4 basil leaves, chopped
Salt and pepper to taste
1 cup green peas
2 tablespoons olive oil
1/2 lemon, juiced
1 pinch chili flakes

Directions:
1. Place the parsnips in a food processor and pulse until ground.
2. Transfer the parsnip into a bowl and stir in the parsley, cilantro and basil, as well as green peas.
3. Add salt, pepper, lemon juice, olive oil and chili flakes and mix gently.
4. Serve the rice fresh.

Cumin Coleslaw

This recipe makes enough for 2-4 servings and it's filling enough to count as a main dish for lunch. It's a delicious dish that combines a wide range of vegetables and offers you a wide array of nutrients at the same time.

Time: 30 minutes
Servings: 2-4

Ingredients:
1 cup shredded red cabbage
1 cup shredded white cabbage
1 zucchini, finely sliced
2 carrots, grated
1/2 head lettuce, shredded
1 1/2 teaspoons cumin seeds
1/2 cup cashew nuts, soaked overnight
2 tablespoons lemon juice
Salt and pepper to taste

1/4 cup water

Directions:
1. Mix the cabbage, zucchini and lettuce in a salad bowl.
2. Combine the cumin seeds, cashew nuts, lemon juice, water, salt and pepper in a blender and pulse until smooth.
3. Spoon the dressing over the coleslaw and mix well.
4. Season the coleslaw with salt and pepper to taste and serve it fresh or store in an airtight container in the fridge for 2 days maximum.

Hemp Butternut Squash Pasta

A bowl of this pasta is rich and filling and the recipe itself is simple so you've got all the reasons to give it a try. In addition to this, it has a mild aroma, comforting for your taste buds.

Time: 30 minutes
Servings: 4

Ingredients:
1/2 butternut squash, peeled
2 garlic cloves
1/2 lemon, juiced
2 tablespoons hemp seeds
1 cup fresh cilantro
2 tablespoons olive oil
Salt and pepper to taste

Directions:
1. Cut the butternut squash with a spiral slicer into fine strips and place them in a bowl.
2. Combine the garlic, lemon juice, hemp seeds, cilantro and olive oil in a blender.
3. Add salt and pepper to taste and pulse until smooth.
4. Spoon the sauce over the butternut squash and mix gently.
5. Adjust the taste with salt and pepper and serve the pasta fresh.

Summer Squash Cold Soup

Summer squash is a great vegetable for soups due to being high in water content. Plus, it has a mild aroma so even the pickiest eaters might enjoy it.

Time: 20 minutes
Servings: 2-4

Ingredients:
4 small summer squashes
2 garlic cloves
1 shallot
1/4 cup olive oil
1 yellow bell pepper, cored
1 jalapeno, seeded
1/2 lemon, juice
1 cup water
Salt and pepper to taste
Chopped cilantro for serving

Directions:
1. Combine the squashes with garlic, shallot, olive oil, lemon juice and water in a blender and pulse until smooth.
2. Add salt and pepper then stir in the bell pepper and jalapeno.

3. Pour the soup into serving bowls and top with chopped cilantro just before serving.

Zucchini Vegetable Rolls

These wraps, using zucchini slices, are refreshing and loaded with the needed nutrients to keep you full until dinner. The wraps are particularly high in fibers and vitamins and make an excellent meal dipped in the cashew herbs sauce.

Time: 30 minutes
Servings: 6

Ingredients:
1 large zucchini
2 carrots, cut into sticks
1 cup shredded cabbage
1 avocado, sliced
2 red bell peppers, cored and sliced
1/4 cup cashew nuts, soaked overnight
1/4 cup chopped cilantro
2 tablespoons chopped parsley
2 garlic cloves
2 tablespoons lemon juice
Salt and pepper to taste
Chives to secure the rolls

Directions:
1. Mix the cashew nuts, cilantro, parsley, garlic, lemon juice, salt and pepper in a blender and pulse until smooth.
2. Add water if the sauce needs to be thinned down and pour the sauce into a bowl. Place it aside.
3. Cut the zucchini in thin slices lengthwise and place each side on your chopping board.
4. Place the carrots, cabbage, avocado and bell peppers on each slice of zucchini and roll tightly. Secure each roll with chives.
5. Serve the rolls dipped into the herbed sauce.

Raw Caesar Salad

The classic Caesar salad is anything but raw and vegan, but worry not since this recipe preserves the flavor of the classic recipe, but in a raw version which is much healthier and just as rich and delicious!

Time: 25 minutes
Servings: 4

Ingredients:
1 head lettuce, shredded
1 head broccoli, cut into small florets
1/2 radicchio, shredded
1/4 cup cashew nuts, soaked overnight
1/4 cup lemon juice
2 garlic cloves
Salt and pepper to taste
2 tablespoons pine nuts

Directions:
1. Place the shredded lettuce, broccoli and radicchio in a salad bowl.
2. To make the dressing, combine the cashews, lemon juice, garlic, salt and pepper in a blender and pulse until smooth.
3. Drizzle the dressing over the lettuce and mix gently until the ingredients are evenly distributed.
4. Serve the salad fresh, topped with pine nuts for texture.

Guacamole Stuffed Tomatoes

Guacamole is such a delicious dip! But if you leave it chunkier it can count as a salad and make an excellent lunch meal. Moreover, stuff some tomatoes with it and you've got yourself a great lunch box dish!

Time: 25 minutes
Servings: 4

Ingredients:
4 medium size tomatoes
2 ripe avocados
2 garlic cloves, minced
2 green onions, chopped
1 cucumber, diced
1 cup chopped spinach
1/4 lemon, juiced
1 jalapeno pepper, chopped
Salt and pepper to taste

Directions:
1. Cut the top of each tomato and carefully remove the flesh and seeds, leaving the tomatoes intact as much as possible.
2. Chop the flesh of the tomatoes and place them aside.
3. To make the guacamole, mash the avocados with a fork then stir in the garlic, green onions, cucumber, spinach, lemon juice and jalapeno. Stir in the chopped tomatoes as well.
4. Add salt and pepper to taste and spoon the guacamole into each tomato.
5. Serve the tomatoes fresh.

Beet Salad with Parsley Pesto

This dish, although names salad, is not the light kind you might imagine. Instead, it is loaded with fibers and so filling that even a small amount is enough to fill you up for lunch.

Time: 30 minutes
Servings: 2

Ingredients:
4 medium size beets, finely grated
2 garlic cloves
1 cup fresh parsley
2/3 cup walnuts
1/4 lemon, juiced
Salt and pepper to taste

Directions:
1. Mix the garlic with parsley, walnuts and lemon juice in a blender.
2. Add salt and pepper to taste and pulse until smooth.
3. Mix the grated beets with walnut pesto in a salad bowl then adjust the taste with salt and pepper if needed.
4. Serve the salad right away.

Spinach Pizza

If you're worried that going raw and vegan means giving up on your favorite pizza, please know that you have plenty of healthy and delicious options, such as this spinach pizza which may not be cooked, but it tastes heavenly.

Time: 6 1/2 hours
Servings: 6

Ingredients:
Crust:
2 cups raw almonds
1 cup ground flax seeds
1 cup water
2 tablespoons olive oil
1 teaspoon Italian herbs
Salt to taste
Topping:
1/4 cup sun-dried tomatoes
1/4 cup hemp seeds
2 tablespoons olive oil
2 cups baby spinach
Salt and pepper to taste

Directions:
1. To make the crust, combine all the ingredients in a powerful blender or food processor and pulse until ground and well mixed.
2. Spread the mixture on your dehydrator pan, as thick as you like and dehydrate at 115F for 6 hours.
3. For the topping, mix the sun-dried tomatoes with hemp seeds, olive oil, salt and pepper in a blender and pulse until smooth.
4. Spread this mixture over the crust and top with baby spinach.
5. Cut into slices and serve the pizza fresh.

Raw Lasagna

Lasagna is a classic dish, but here is a raw version that tastes just as good as the classic, despite replacing most of its layers with their raw counterparts.

Time: 1 hour
Servings: 10

Ingredients:
4 young zucchinis, thinly sliced lengthwise
2 cups macadamia nuts, soaked overnight
1/4 cup pine nuts
2 tablespoons lemon juice
1 teaspoon dried Italian herbs
Salt and pepper to taste
1/4 cup water
3 Portobello mushrooms, finely sliced
4 cups baby spinach, shredded
1 cup sun-dried tomatoes, soaked for 2 hours
4 dates, pitted
2 garlic cloves
2 cups diced tomatoes
2 tablespoons olive oil

Directions:
1. Mix the macadamia nuts with pine nuts, lemon juice, herbs, salt, pepper and water in a food processor and pulse until smooth. Place aside.
2. Combine the sun-dried tomatoes, dates, garlic, diced tomatoes and olive oil in a blender and pulse until smooth. Add salt and pepper to taste.
3. Take a deep dish bowl and layer the zucchini slices, macadamia mixture, mushrooms, spinach and tomato sauce in the bowl.
4. Serve the lasagna fresh.

Hot and Sour Green Salad

If you like spicy food, this salad is for you. The sour dressing and the hot red pepper make an excellent team and balance the final taste of the salad perfectly.

Time: 25 minutes
Servings: 2

Ingredients:
1 bag mixed greens
2 green onions, coarsely chopped
1/2 head broccoli, cut into fine florets
1 red pepper, seeded and sliced
2 tablespoons lemon juice
1 tablespoon raw coconut aminos
1 teaspoon grated ginger
1/2 teaspoon sesame oil
2 tablespoons lemon juice
2 tablespoons sesame seeds
1/4 cup raw peanuts, chopped

Directions:
1. Mix the mixed greens and onions in a bowl.
2. To make the dressing, combine the red pepper, rice vinegar, balsamic vinegar, coconut aminos, ginger, sesame oil and lemon juice in a glass jar and seal it with a lid.
3. Shake the jar well then drizzle the dressing over the salad.
4. Mix gently.
5. Top the salad with sesame seeds and peanuts before serving.

Cooked Dinner Recipes

Vegan Coconut Curry

Curry, despite having Oriental origins, has become an International dish in the last few years, spreading to every single continent. People love its aroma, its heat and texture and in addition to that, it is also a versatile dish.

Time: 30 minutes
Servings: 4-6

Ingredients:
1 tablespoon coconut oil
1 shallot, chopped
4 garlic cloves, chopped
1 teaspoon grated ginger
2 tablespoons red curry paste
1 cup coconut milk
2 cups vegetable stock

1 head cauliflower, cut into florets
1 cup canned chickpeas, drained
1/4 pound baby carrots
1/2 cup snow peas
Salt and pepper to taste
Chopped cilantro for serving

Directions:
1. Heat the oil in a heavy pot. Stir in the shallot, garlic and ginger and cook for 2 minutes until soft and translucent.
2. Add the curry paste and coconut milk, as well as stock and bring the mixture to a boil.
3. Stir in the cauliflower, chickpeas, baby carrots and snow peas then add salt and pepper to taste.
4. Cook the curry on medium flame for 20 minutes.
5. Serve the curry warm, topped with chopped cilantro, over boiled rice if you prefer.

Roasted Vegetable Salad with Spicy Dressing

Roasting vegetables enhances their natural sweetness so the spicy dressing is the perfect match for the sweet, smoky veggies. The final dish is well balanced and absolutely delicious!

Time: 30 minutes
Servings: 4

Ingredients:
1 zucchini, sliced
1 eggplant, peeled and sliced
1 bunch young fresh carrots
1 bunch beet greens
4 garlic cloves, minced
2 tablespoons olive oil
3 tablespoons balsamic vinegar
1/2 teaspoon chili flakes
1/4 teaspoon cumin seeds
Salt and pepper to taste

Directions:
1. Heat a grill pan over medium flame. Place the zucchinis, eggplant, carrots and beet greens, one at a time, on the grill and cook on each side until browned and tender.
2. Transfer the vegetables into a salad bowl.
3. For the dressing, mix the garlic, olive oil, balsamic vinegar, chili flakes, cumin seeds, salt and pepper in a glass jar. Seal the jar with a lid and shake well until smooth.
4. Drizzle the dressing over the salad and serve it fresh.

Vegan Mac'n'Cheese

Mac and cheese is not precisely a low calorie dish if made the traditional way. But this recipe manages to pull out a dish that is not only lower in calories, but also delicious, preserving the same aroma and texture of mac and cheese.

Time: 30 minutes
Servings: 4

Ingredients:
12 oz. gluten-free short pasta
1 shallot, chopped
2 garlic cloves, minced
1 cup cashew nuts, soaked overnight
1 cup vegetable stock
1/2 teaspoon cumin powder
1/4 teaspoon chili powder
2 tablespoons nutritional yeast
Salt and pepper to taste

Directions:
1. Pour a few cups of water in a large pot and bring it to a boil with a pinch of salt.
2. Add the pasta and cook 8-10 minutes until al dente. Drain the pasta well and place it in a deep dish baking pan.
3. To make the cheese sauce, mix the cashews with shallot, garlic, stock, cumin powder, chili powder and nutritional yeast in a blender.
4. Pulse until smooth then season with salt and pepper and pour the sauce over the pasta.
5. Mix well then place the pan in the preheated oven at 350F for 15 minutes.
6. Serve the dish warm.

Roasted Cauliflower and Brussels Sprouts

Brussels sprouts may not be your first choice when it comes to delicious veggies, but they are incredibly versatile and if cooked properly just as delicious. The key is to not overcook them. If they preserve part of their crunch, they taste so much better!

Time: 30 minutes
Servings: 4

Ingredients:
1/2 head cauliflower, cut into florets
1 pound Brussels sprouts, halved
2 tablespoons olive oil
2 garlic cloves, sliced
1/2 lemon, juiced
Salt and pepper to taste

Directions:
1. Mix the cauliflower Brussels sprouts in a baking tray.
2. Combine the olive oil, garlic and lemon juice in a small bowl. Add salt and pepper to taste and drizzle this mixture over the sprouts and cauliflower.
3. Mix gently to evenly distribute the ingredients.
4. Roast in the preheated oven at 350F for 20 minutes.
5. Serve the vegetables warm.

Quinoa Chickpea Salad

Quinoa is known as the "supergrain of the future" due to its high nutritional content, but apart from being healthy, it's also easy to cook and easy to combine with a wide array of vegetables, including chickpeas and plenty of herbs.

Time: 30 minutes
Servings: 2-4

Ingredients:
2/3 cup dry quinoa, rinsed
2 1/2 cups vegetable stock
1 can chickpeas, drained
1 cup cherry tomatoes, halved
1 ripe avocado, sliced
2 cups baby spinach
1 small red onion, sliced
1 lemon, juiced
1 teaspoon lemon zest
1 tablespoon Dijon mustard
2 tablespoons olive oil
1 teaspoon maple syrup
1/4 teaspoon cumin powder
Salt and pepper to taste
2 tablespoons chopped parsley
2 tablespoons chopped cilantro

Directions:
1. Combine the quinoa with the stock in a saucepan and cook over low to medium flame until most of the liquid is absorbed.
2. Transfer the quinoa in a salad bowl then add the chickpeas, tomatoes, avocado, baby spinach and red onion.
3. For the dressing, mix the lemon juice, lemon zest, mustard, olive oil, maple syrup, cumin powder, salt and pepper and mix well.
4. Drizzle the dressing over the quinoa and mix gently to evenly distribute it.
5. Add the parsley and cilantro and serve the salad fresh.

Millet Spinach Soup

Many people prefer soups for dinner and who can blame them?! A bowl of warm, hearty soup can fix anything that went wrong during the day and it will get you back on track right away, moreover when the soup is as healthy and delicious as this one.

Time: 30 minutes
Servings: 4-6

Ingredients:
2 tablespoons olive oil
1 sweet onion, chopped
1 large carrot, diced
1 celery stalk, diced
1 zucchini, diced
2 garlic cloves, chopped
1 can diced tomatoes
5 cups vegetable stock
1/2 teaspoon dried basil
1/2 teaspoon dried oregano
1/2 teaspoon dried thyme
1 cup millet, rinsed
2 cups baby spinach
2 tablespoons chopped parsley

Directions:
1. Heat the olive oil in a soup pot and stir in the onion, carrot, celery, zucchini and garlic.
2. Sauté for 2 minutes then add the diced tomatoes, stock and herbs.
3. Bring the soup to a boil and cook for 5 minutes, adjusting the taste with salt and pepper.
4. Add the millet and cook the soup 20 additional minutes.
5. Remove from heat and stir in the spinach and parsley.
6. Serve the soup warm or freeze it in individual airtight containers.

Quinoa Edamame Salad

Edamame is not as known as green peas or other green vegetables, but it's amazing in terms of taste and nutrients and it makes a nice change from the usual salads, especially combined with the healthy quinoa.

Time: 30 minutes
Servings: 4

Ingredients:
3/4 cup quinoa, rinsed
2 cups vegetable stock
2 tablespoons olive oil
1 shallot, sliced
2 garlic cloves, chopped
1 red bell pepper, cored and sliced
2 cups shelled frozen edamame
3 tablespoons lemon juice
1 teaspoon dried mixed herbs
Salt and pepper to taste

Directions:
1. Mix the quinoa with stock in a saucepan and cook until all the liquid is absorbed.
2. In the meantime, heat the oil in a skillet and stir in the shallot, garlic and bell pepper. Sauté for 2 minutes then add the edamame.
3. Cook for 10 minutes, stirring often then remove from heat and transfer into a salad bowl.
4. Add the cooked quinoa, lemon juice, herbs, salt and pepper and mix well.
5. Serve the salad fresh, warm or chilled.

Roasted Bell Pepper Millet Stew

This saucy stew is incredibly easy to make, but the taste is unique and divine. The key to the final aroma of this stew are the roasted bell pepper which are slightly smoky and sweet. A bowl of this and your taste buds are in heaven!

Time: 30 minutes
Servings: 4

Ingredients:
1 tablespoon olive oil
1 red onion, sliced
2 garlic cloves, minced
4 roasted bell peppers, shredded
1 cup diced tomatoes
2 tablespoons tomato paste
1 cup millet
2 1/2 cups vegetable stock
Salt and pepper to taste
1 bay leaf
1 spring thyme

Directions:
1. Heat the oil in a heavy saucepan and stir in the red onion and garlic.
2. Sauté for 2 minutes then add the bell peppers, followed by the tomatoes and tomato paste.
3. Bring the mixture to a boil then stir in the millet, stock, bay leaf, thyme, salt and pepper.
4. Cook the stew for 20 minutes and serve it warm or store in the fridge in an airtight container for up to 2 days.

Baked Herbed Falafels

Falafel is a well-known Oriental dish and just like curry, it uses spices to create a bold aroma and a delicious bite. What I love about this recipe is that it can be made ahead of time and served either warm or chilled.

Time: 30 minutes
Servings: 6

Ingredients:
1 15-oz. can chickpeas, drained
4 garlic cloves, minced
1 shallot, chopped
1 tablespoon chopped cilantro
2 tablespoons chopped parsley
1/2 cup cooked quinoa
2 tablespoons ground flax seeds
6 tablespoons cold water
1 tablespoon olive oil
Salt and pepper to taste

Directions:
1. Mix the ground flaxseeds with cold water and let them soak up for a few minutes.

2. Combine the chickpeas with garlic, shallot, cilantro, parsley and quinoa in a bowl and pulse until ground.
3. Add the flaxseeds and mix until the mixture comes together.
4. Season with salt and pepper then form small patties and place them on a baking tray lined with parchment paper.
5. Cook in the preheated oven at 350F for 15 minutes or until slightly golden brown.
6. Serve the falafel warm or chilled.

Vegetable Buckwheat Salad

Couscous, unlike other grains, is much easier to cook and with less hassle so you can quickly make this dish for dinner and please your entire family.

Time: 20 minutes
Servings: 4-6

Ingredients:
1 cup buckwheat
2 cups hot vegetable stock
1/2 teaspoon turmeric powder
1 red bell pepper, cored and sliced
1 yellow bell pepper, cored and sliced
1/2 fennel bulb, sliced
1 zucchini, sliced
2 cups butternut squash cubes
1 cup cherry tomatoes
1/4 cup chopped parsley
1 tablespoon olive oil
1 lemon, juiced
Salt and pepper to taste

Directions:
1. Mix the buckwheat and stock in a saucepan and cook it over low to medium flame for 20 minutes or until all the liquid has been absorbed.
2. In the meantime, heat a grill pan over medium to high flame and place the bell peppers, zucchinis, squash and cherry tomatoes on the grill. Cook them on all sides until browned.
3. Transfer the cooked buckwheat into a salad bowl then add the grilled vegetables, parsley, lemon juice and olive oil.
4. Season with salt and pepper and mix gently in the bowl to evenly distribute the ingredients.
5. Serve the salad warm or chilled.

Tomato Caper Linguine

This tomato caper sauce is so easy to make and yet so delicious! But with its simplicity it brings the linguine to a whole new level of deliciousness and makes a filling, nutritious meal for dinner.

Time: 30 minutes
Servings: 4

Ingredients:
1 tablespoon olive oil
2 garlic cloves, chopped
1 shallot, sliced
1/2 teaspoon chili flakes
2 cups tomato sauce
1 cup diced tomatoes
1 jalapeno pepper, chopped
2 teaspoons capers, chopped
12 oz. gluten-free linguine
Salt and pepper to taste

Directions:
1. Pour a few cups of water in a pot and bring it to a boil with a pinch of salt. Add the linguine and cook them for 8-10 minutes or until al dente. Drain and place into a bowl.
2. For the sauce, heat the oil in a saucepan. Add the garlic and shallot and cook for 2 minutes then stir in the chili flakes, tomato sauce, diced tomatoes, jalapeno and capers.
3. Adjust the taste with salt and pepper and cook the sauce for 15 minutes on low heat.
4. Pour the sauce over the linguine and mix well. Serve the pasta warm.

Baked Potatoes with Avocado Garlic Sauce

This dish is the proof that simplicity is the best path to delicious dishes! It may have only a few ingredients but the final result exceeds any expectation in terms of aroma and texture!

Time: 50 minutes
Servings: 4

Ingredients:
4 large potatoes, washed
1 small avocado
4 garlic cloves
1/2 lemon, juiced
Salt and pepper to taste

Directions:
1. Place the potatoes in a large pot and cover them with water. Add a pinch of salt and bring the water to a boil.
2. Cook the potatoes for 20 minutes until a knife inserted in the potatoes goes through easily.

3. Drain the potatoes and place them in a baking tray.
4. Crush the potatoes with the bottom of a saucepan and cook them in the preheated oven at 350F for 20 additional minute.
5. For the sauce, mix the avocado, garlic, lemon juice, salt and pepper in a blender and pulse until smooth.
6. Drizzle the avocado garlic sauce over the baked potatoes and serve them warm.

Quinoa Kale Cakes

These cakes can be served either simple or with a garlic sauce, in sandwiches or in lettuce wraps. They are healthy and packed with protein, good fats and fibers so they make an excellent dinner.

Time: 40 minutes
Servings: 6

Ingredients:
1 1/2 cups cooked quinoa
2 tablespoons ground flax seeds
6 tablespoons cold water
1 cup finely chopped kale
1 medium size sweet potato, finely grated
1/4 cup sunflower seeds
2 tablespoons coconut flour
2 garlic cloves, minced
2 tablespoons tahini paste
Salt and pepper to taste

Directions:
1. Combine all the ingredients in a bowl and mix well, adjusting the taste with salt and pepper.
2. Form small patties and place them on a baking tray lined with parchment paper.
3. Bake in the preheated oven at 350F for 20 minutes.
4. Serve the quinoa cakes warm or chilled.

Amaranth Tabbouleh

Tabbouleh is a classic Oriental salad, but unlike other dishes from that side of the world it doesn't contain a mix of spices. Instead, it relies on fresh herbs to bring in the flavor and nutrients. This particular recipe replaces the couscous with amaranth which is an ancient grain with amazing health benefits.

Time: 30 minutes
Servings: 4

Ingredients:
1/2 cup amaranth
1 1/2 cups hot vegetable stock
1/4 cup hemp seeds
1 cup chopped parsley
4 mint leaves, chopped
2 cups cherry tomatoes, halved
2 celery stalks, sliced
2 cucumbers, sliced
Salt and pepper to taste
3 tablespoons lemon juice

Directions:
1. Combine the amaranth with stock in a saucepan and cook over medium flame for 20 minutes or until the liquid has been absorbed.
2. Mix the hemp seeds, parsley, tomatoes, celery and cucumber in a salad bowl. Stir in the cooked amaranth.
3. Add lemon juice and season with salt and pepper to taste.
4. Mix gently to evenly distribute the flavors and serve the tabbouleh fresh.

Portobello Steaks with Sautéed Vegetables

The flavors of this dish are simple in their essence and the combination itself is a classic, but that means one thing – even the pickiest eaters will love this protein packed dish.

Time: 30 minutes
Servings: 4

Ingredients:
4 Portobello mushrooms
1 tablespoon vegetable oil
1 zucchini, sliced
2 carrots, cut into sticks
1 celery stalk, cut into stick'
2 small eggplants, peeled and sliced
Salt and pepper to taste
1 tablespoon coconut aminos
1 teaspoon dried oregano

Directions:
1. Heat a grill pan over medium flame. Season the mushrooms with salt and pepper and place them on the grill.
2. Cook the mushrooms on both sides until browned.
3. While the mushrooms cook, heat the oil in a frying pan.
4. Add the zucchini, carrots, celery and eggplant. Cook on medium flame for 10-15 minutes, stirring often.
5. Season with salt and pepper then stir in the coconut aminos and oregano.
6. Serve the grilled mushrooms topped with sautéed vegetables.

Vegetable "Meatloaf"

Despite its name, this dish has no meat in its composition. Instead, it has vegetables, walnuts, mushrooms and plenty of spices so the final loaf is juicy and flavorful.

Time: 1 1/2 hours
Servings: 6-8

Ingredients:
2 tablespoons olive oil
2 garlic cloves, minced
1 shallot, chopped
1 red bell pepper, diced
1 yellow bell pepper, diced
2 pounds cremini mushrooms, chopped
1 cup green peas
1 cup walnuts, ground
2 tablespoons coconut flour
1 tablespoon Dijon mustard
1 tablespoon tomato paste
2 tablespoons nutritional yeast
Salt and pepper to taste
2 tablespoons ground flaxseeds
6 tablespoons cold water

Directions:
1. Mix the ground flaxseeds with cold water and let them soak up for 10 minutes.
2. Heat the oil in a skillet and stir in the garlic and shallot. Sauté for 2 minutes then stir in bell peppers and mushrooms.
3. Cook for10 minutes, stirring often then remove from heat and transfer into a large bowl.
4. Add the soaked flaxseeds, green peas, walnuts, coconut flour, mustard, tomato paste and nutritional yeast.
5. Season with salt and pepper and mix well then spoon the mixture into a greased loaf pan.
6. Bake in the preheated oven at 350F for 45 minutes.
7. Let the "meatloaf" cool in the pan before serving.

Mushroom Millet Risotto

Risotto is an Italian dish that shines in its simplicity! The mushrooms add so much depth of flavor and make this dish even more filling and nutritious.

Time: 30 minutes
Servings: 4

Ingredients:
3/4 cup millet
2 cups vegetable stock, warm
1 tablespoon olive oil
1 shallot, chopped
4 Portobello mushrooms, diced
1/2 teaspoon dried basil
1/4 cup coconut milk
Salt and pepper to taste
1 tablespoon nutritional yeast

Directions:
1. Heat the oil in a heavy saucepan. Stir in the shallot and sauté for 1 minute then add the mushrooms and cook for 5 minutes.
2. Stir in the millet then gradually stir in the stock, 1/2 cup at a time. Don't add a new batch of stock before seeing that the previous batch has been absorbed into the risotto.
3. When you run out of stock, stir in the basil and coconut milk and adjust the taste with salt and pepper.
4. Remove the risotto from heat and stir in the nutritional yeast.
5. Serve the risotto warm.

Tomato Chili

Chili is famous for its heat and this recipe makes no exception! It's such a filling and rich stew, perfect for dinner for the entire family.

Time: 40 minutes
Servings: 4-6

Ingredients:
1 tablespoon olive oil
1 red onion, chopped
4 garlic cloves, chopped
2 jalapeno peppers, chopped
1 teaspoon cumin seeds
1 teaspoon paprika
2 cups vegetable stock
1 can diced tomatoes
1 can kidney beans, drained
1 can pinto beans, drained
Salt and pepper to taste
2 green onions, chopped
2 tablespoons chopped parsley

Directions:
1. Heat the oil in a heavy pot and stir in the red onion, garlic and jalapeno. Sauté for 2 minutes.
2. Stir in the remaining ingredients, except green onions and parsley.
3. Season the chili with salt and pepper and cook over medium flame for 30 minutes.
4. When almost done, stir in the green onions and parsley and serve the chili warm.

Spiced Lentil Stew

This stew combines the mild lentils with spices and manages to create a rich, fragrant, saucy stew to serve at dinner for the entire family.

Time: 50 minutes
Servings: 4-6

Ingredients:
1 cup red lentils, rinsed
3 cups water
1 bay leaf
2 tablespoons olive oil
1 red onion, chopped
2 garlic cloves, chopped
1 teaspoon curry powder
1 cup diced tomatoes
1/2 teaspoon cumin powder
1/2 teaspoon cayenne pepper
1/4 teaspoon dried thyme
Salt and pepper to taste
2 tablespoons chopped parsley

Directions:
1. Mix the red lentils with water and bay leaf in a saucepan and cook for 20 minutes. Drain and discard the bay leaf.
2. Heat the oil in a heavy saucepan and stir in the red onion and garlic. Sauté for 2 minutes then add the curry powder, tomatoes, cumin powder, cayenne pepper, thyme, salt and pepper.
3. Stir in the drained lentils and cook the stew for 20 minutes.
4. Stir in the parsley and serve the stew warm.

Quinoa Cauliflower Salad

If you're looking for a lighter meal for dinner, this is the recipe to go for! It's simple and the flavor profile is mild, but the final dish is nutritious and makes an excellent choice for your late dinner.

Time: 30 minutes
Servings: 4

Ingredients:
Salad:
1/2 cup quinoa
1 1/2 cups vegetable stock
1 pinch saffron strands
1/2 cauliflower head, cut into florets
1 cup green peas
1/4 cup chopped cilantro
Salt and pepper to taste
2 tablespoons lemon juice
Dressing:
1/2 avocado
2 garlic cloves
2 tablespoons lemon juice
Salt and pepper to taste

Directions:
1. Mix the quinoa, stock and saffron strands in a saucepan and cook for 15 minutes or until the liquid has been absorbed.
2. Transfer the quinoa into a salad bowl and stir in the cauliflower florets, green peas, cilantro, lemon juice, salt and pepper.
3. Mix the salad gently to evenly distribute the ingredients.
4. For the dressing, combine all the ingredients in a blender. Pulse until smooth and creamy.
5. Top the salad with avocado dressing just before serving.

Caraway Cabbage and Broccoli

Although this dish is incredibly simple, the flavors are amazing. If you haven't tried caraway seeds before, you definitely should. You'll be impressed by its intense flavor and how well it complements cabbage.

Time: 25 minutes
Servings: 2-4

Ingredients:
1 small head cabbage, shredded
1 head broccoli, cut into florets
2 tablespoons vegetable oil
1 sweet onion, sliced
1 teaspoon caraway seeds
1 small red pepper, seeded and sliced
Salt and pepper to taste

Directions:
1. Heat the oil in a large saucepan and stir in the onion. Sauté for 2 minutes until soft and translucent.
2. Add the caraway seeds and cook them 1 minute until they begin to pop, then stir in the cabbage and broccoli.
3. Sauté the dish over medium flame, stirring often, for 10 minutes or until most of the liquid evaporates and the cabbage and broccoli become tender.
4. Remove from heat and stir in the red pepper, as well as salt and pepper to taste.
5. Serve the dish warm.

Pumpkin Curry Stew

Although pumpkin is more known for its sweet dishes, it also makes excellent savory main meals and this curry is the perfect example of a pumpkin dish that balances its natural sweetness and spices well.

Time: 40 minutes
Servings: 4

Ingredients:
4 cups pumpkin cubes
1 tablespoon olive oil
3 tablespoons red curry paste
1 sweet onion, chopped
1 teaspoon mustard seeds
4 cardamom pods, crushed
1 1/2 cups coconut milk
1 cup vegetable stock
Salt and pepper to taste
1 lime, juiced
2 tablespoons chopped cilantro
4 mint leaves, chopped

Directions:

1. Heat the olive oil in a heavy saucepan and stir in the curry paste, onion, mustard seeds and cardamom.
2. Cook for 2 minutes then add the pumpkin cubes, coconut milk and stock.
3. Season with salt and pepper and cook the stew for320 minutes, avoiding to stir too often as it crushes the pumpkin cubes.
4. Stir in the lime juice, cilantro and mint and remove from heat.
5. Serve the stew warm. For a festive or impressive look, serve the stew in an empty, carved pumpkin.

Lentil Tomato Ragu

Ragu is a versatile Italian dish usually served with pasta, but it's so versatile that it can be served and used in other dishes as well. You can freeze it in individual container and store it for up to 2 months in the freezer. This way you know you have a serving of ragu whenever your cooking time is short.

Time: 1 hour
Servings: 8-10

Ingredients:
1 tablespoon olive oil
1 large onion, finely chopped
2 carrots, grated
2 celery stalks, chopped
2 garlic cloves, chopped
2 cups red lentils
2 cans diced tomatoes
1 teaspoon dried basil
1 teaspoon dried oregano
1 sprig thyme
1 bay leaf
4 cups vegetable stock
Salt and pepper to taste

Directions:
1. Heat the olive oil in a large heavy saucepan. Stir in the onion and cook for 2 minutes until soft and translucent.
2. Add the carrots, celery, garlic and lentils and cook 5 additional minutes.
3. Stir in the remaining ingredients and season with salt and pepper.
4. Cook the ragu over low heat, stirring occasionally, for 40 minutes or until the lentils are tender and saucy.
5. Serve the ragu warm , with pasta, or freeze it until needed.

Bean and Tomato Casserole

Casseroles are incredible because you can throw some ingredients in a deep pan and leave the oven do the rest of the work. But then you get to enjoy a delicious and filling dish!

Time: 1 hour
Servings: 6-8

Ingredients:
2 cans white beans, drained
1 sweet onion, sliced
2 garlic cloves, minced
2 carrots, diced
4 ripe tomatoes, cubed
1 cup tomato sauce
Salt and pepper to taste
1/2 teaspoon hot sauce
1/2 teaspoon cumin seeds

Directions:
1. Combine all the ingredients in a deep dish baking pan.
2. Adjust the taste with salt and pepper and cook the casserole in the preheated oven at 350F for 35 minutes.
3. Serve the casserole warm or chilled.

Vegetable Soup with Pesto Dressing

Who would have thought that pesto makes such an excellent dressing for soup?! It just brings a simple vegetable soup to a whole new level of deliciousness and fragrance!

Time: 1 hour
Servings: 4-6

Ingredients:
1 tablespoon olive oil
2 leeks, sliced
2 cups green beans, cut in large chunks
1 zucchini, diced
2 cups water
3 cups vegetable stock
4 ripe tomatoes, peeled and diced
Salt and pepper to taste
1/4 cup quinoa
1/2 cup fresh basil leaves
2 tablespoons pine nuts
1 tablespoon olive oil
2 garlic cloves

Directions:
1. Heat the olive oil in a soup pot and stir in the leeks. Sauté for 5-7 minutes until soft then add the green beans, zucchini, water, stock and tomatoes.
2. Season with salt and pepper and bring the soup to a boil. Cook over medium flame for 20 minutes.
3. Stir in the quinoa and cook 15 additional minutes.
4. To make the pesto, combine the basil, pine nuts, olive oil, garlic and a pinch of salt in a mortar. Using a pestle, mix until you obtain a smooth paste.
5. When the soup is done, pour it into serving bowls and top it with a few drops of freshly made pesto. Serve right away.

Warm Spinach Salad with Raisins and Pine Nuts

This warm salad is the perfect mix between healthy and delicious, but also comforting. It combines a wide range of ingredients, each with its unique aroma and nutrients, but it manages to bring them together nicely.

Time: 30 minutes
Servings: 4

Ingredients:
2 tablespoons olive oil
2 garlic cloves, crushed
4 cups baby spinach
1/2 cup golden raisins
1/4 cup pine nuts
1/2 lemon, juiced
Salt and pepper to taste

Directions:
1. Heat the oil in a skillet and add the garlic. Cook just until the garlic begins to turn golden brown then remove and discard the garlic.
2. Place the pan back over medium flame and heat the oil once more.
3. Stir in the spinach and cook for 10 minutes until the liquid begins to evaporate.
4. Add the raisins, pine nuts, lemon juice, as well as salt and pepper and mix over medium flame for 2 additional minutes.
5. Serve the salad right away.

Butternut Squash and Tomato Gratin

Rich butternut squash, fragrant basil and juicy tomatoes come together into this brilliant, delicious casserole dish, making it irresistible.

Time: 1 hour
Servings: 6-8

Ingredients:
1 tablespoon olive oil
1 sweet onion, sliced
1 small butternut squash, peeled and cut into thin slices
2 cups tomato sauce
1 can diced tomatoes
1/2 teaspoon chili flakes
1 teaspoon dried basil
2 tablespoons nutritional yeast
Salt and pepper to taste

Directions:
1. Grease a deep baking pan with olive oil.
2. Place the onion slices at the bottom of the pan and top it with butternut squash slices.
3. Mix the tomato sauce with diced tomatoes, chili flakes, basil and nutritional yeast in a bowl. Add salt and pepper then pour this mixture over the butternut squash.
4. Cook the gratin in the preheated oven at 350F for 45 minutes.
5. Serve the gratin warm.

Quinoa Kale Pilaf

Pilaf is traditional for Eastern Europe and it is a rich, filling dish made with anything, from root vegetables to spring veggies. It's a versatile dish and this particular recipe uses kale to create a healthy, nutritious meal for your dinner.

Time: 40 minutes
Servings: 4

Ingredients:
1 tablespoon olive oil
1 shallot, chopped
2 garlic cloves, minced
8 oz. mushrooms, sliced
4 ripe tomatoes, diced
1 cup dry quinoa, rinsed
3 cups vegetable stock
Salt and pepper to taste
1 bay leaf

Directions:
1. Heat the oil in a heavy saucepan and stir in the shallot and garlic. Sauté for 2 minutes until soft and translucent.
2. Add the mushrooms and keep cooking for 5 minutes then stir in the tomatoes, followed by the quinoa, stock, bay leaf, salt and pepper.
3. Cook the pilaf over low to medium flame for 30 minutes or until most of the liquid has been absorbed.
4. Serve the pilaf warm.

Ginger Chickpea Stew

Although the combination sounds unusual at a first glance, it's definitely worth a try. The ginger brings balance to this dish with its heat and intense fragrant and it makes an excellent team with the chickpeas and spinach.

Time: 1 hour
Servings: 4

Ingredients:
2 teaspoons grated ginger
1 tablespoon olive oil
1 shallot, chopped
4 garlic cloves, chopped
1 teaspoon smoked paprika
1 can diced tomatoes
1 can chickpeas, drained
10 oz. fresh spinach, shredded
Salt and pepper to taste

Directions:
1. Heat the oil in a heavy saucepan and stir in the shallot, garlic and ginger. Sauté for 2 minutes then add the remaining ingredients, except the spinach.
2. Season the stew with salt and pepper as needed and cook it over medium flame for 25 minutes.
3. Stir in the spinach and cook 5 additional minutes then remove from heat and serve the stew warm.

Asian Style Cauliflower Salad

If you prefer Asian flavors, this recipe is for you! The cauliflower is mild enough to take plenty of Asian spices so the final dish is flavorful, but not at all heavy for your stomach.

Time: 30 minutes
Servings: 4

Ingredients:
1 large head cauliflower, cut into florets
2 bok choys shredded
2 tablespoons raw coconut aminos
1/2 teaspoon sesame oil
1/4 cup water
1 red pepper, sliced
1/4 cup sesame seeds
1/4 cup coconut flakes
Salt and pepper to taste
2 tablespoons lemon juice

Directions:
1. Place the cauliflower florets and bok choys in a large bowl.
2. Mix the coconut aminos, sesame oil, water and red pepper in a bowl. Pour this mixture over the cauliflower and mix until evenly coated.
3. Spread the cauliflower and bok choy over a baking tray and sprinkle with sesame seeds and coconut flakes.
4. Season with a touch of salt and freshly ground pepper.
5. Cook in the preheated oven at 350F for 20 minutes.
6. Transfer the cauliflower and bok choy in a salad bowl and drizzle them with lemon juice before serving.

Conclusion

The Raw Until 4 diet goes beyond the lines of a regular diet. It's not as restrictive as other diets and you don't have to count calories. In fact, you can eat anything as long as it's raw and you are also allowed a high carb cooked food. That is enough to make it a desirable diet and one that is fairly easy to follow if you love to eat raw fruits and vegetables. Of course, it can become challenging at time, but what a diet would be without putting your determination and will to test. Luckily, with the RT4 diet, your efforts are paid back and you're not endangering your health for a single second through the process. Weight loss, better general health, fit body and a better state of mind are amongst the benefits of this diet. So wait no more and do the change now! There's not better day than today! Not tomorrow, not in 2 weeks time, don't postpone it, don't avoid it! Keep your mind strong and push yourself over the limit and you will succeed. Because there's nothing you cannot do if you put your mind to it! Embrace this diet with open heart and faith into its guidelines, keep your thoughts positive and optimistic and the goal is easy to reach!

Thank you again for purchasing this book!
Finally, if you've enjoyed this book, then I'd like to ask you for a favor; would you be kind enough to leave a review for this book on Amazon? It would be greatly appreciated!

Click here to leave a review for this book on Amazon!

Bonus: Get Lots Of Valuable Information & A FREE Copy Of:

The 3 "Health" Foods You Need To Stop Eating!

Check Out My Other Books

Below you'll find some of my other popular books that are popular on Amazon and Kindle as well. Simply click on the links below to check them out. Alternatively, you can visit my author page on Amazon to see other work done by me.

Vegan Kids Box Set: Vegan Recipes For Kids & Vegan Diet For Kids

Build Muscle on the Raw Vegan Diet: How to Gain Muscle Mass and Stay Fit on the Raw Food Diet

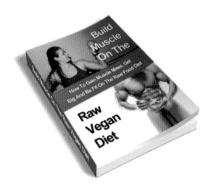

Food Addiction: How To Develop Self Discipline, Control Your Eating And Overcome Food Addiction

Anti Aging From Within: How To Look Younger And Slow Down The Aging Process Naturally and Economically

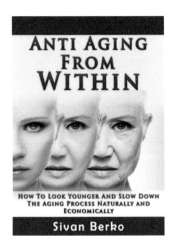

If the links do not work, for whatever reason, you can simply search for these titles on the Amazon website to find them.

Printed in Great Britain
by Amazon.co.uk, Ltd.,
Marston Gate.